Women of Valour Series VIII

"Preparation and Decisions"

Dr. Allison Wiley
and
WOV Contributors

Women of Valour Series VIII

"Preparation and Decisions"
*Dr. Allison Wiley
& WOV Contributors*

Copyright © 2024

All rights reserved. No part of this publication may be reproduced, stored in a retrieval system, or transmitted in any form by any means, for example, electronic, photocopy, recording, scanning, or other without prior written permission of the publisher. The only exception is brief quotations in printed reviews.

CONTENTS

January..Page 5
Dr. Allison Wiley
Prophetess Hope McDowell- Gibson

February..Page 34
Elder Nesa Smith

March..Page 56
Dr. Althea Winifred

April..Page 70
Evangelist Wilma Walker

May...Page 80
Michelle Smith

June..Page 92
Lady Tammy Stewart

July..Page 102
Sharonda Thomas

August...Page 114
Jennifer Lewin

September......................................Page 123
Prophetess Tashana Pearson

October..Page 134
Reverend Sharnelle Jones

November......................................Page 149
Dr. Allison Wiley

December......................................Page 155
Elder Patricia Wright

January

Dr. Allison Wiley

Meet Dr. Allison Wiley

Dr. Allison Wiley is the Founder of Women of Valour, a mandate prophetically spoken into her life in 2016. GOD has called Dr. Wiley to inspire women to fight life's battles by standing firmly on The Promises of GOD.

Dr. Wiley believes Women of Valour will be a catalyst for revival in The Kingdom of GOD. She is an ordained Evangelist and the author of LIFTED.

"And I say also unto thee, That thou art Peter, and upon this rock I will build my church; and the gates of hell shall not prevail against it."
- **Mathew 16:18**

The American pulpit must change. Too much showmanship and flesh. Too many people pleasers standing on top of it. I never thought I would witness "one of our own" turn The Lord's House into a nightclub on New Year's Eve. Falsely supporting the error you can be in the world and have The Church. But yet testifying, souls were saved. Well, put this in the testimony. You deceived these precious ones into thinking they can have both. You just added a lukewarm soul into The Kingdom. That's the message you made VIRAL!

Sad to say, many Christians exposed their hearts in this situation. Proclaiming we should mind our own business and it's the leader's church. Let him run it. Really? Is it? Is the church ours? Did we die for it? Are we the ones who brought it into existence on The Day of Pentecost? Jesus told Apostle Peter, I will build MY CHURCH.

Thank GOD, when the enemy tries to pull The Church down, we have the promise that hell won't win. Glory be to GOD! The Lord's Church will prevail.

While writing I heard this....
To the sheep, I heard the word MIGRATION. For you know the voice of The Shepherd and you must follow it. Start looking for God's Holy Sanctuaries. Leave leaders who are leading you astray. Decide this TODAY.
To the uncompromising leaders, God is about to show you whose Church it really is. I heard The Spirit of The Lord saying PREPARE TO LEAD THE MISLED. They're coming!

Thank you FATHER. Let it be done. Let it be so. In Jesus Name. Amen.

"And when He opened the third seal, I heard the third living creature saying, Come. And I saw, and behold, a black horse; and he who sits on it had a balance in his hand. And I heard as it were a voice in the midst of the four living creatures saying: A choenix of wheat for a denarius and three choenixes of barley for a denarius; and do not harm the oil and the wine"
- Revelation 6:5-6

Greece took my breath away. I give God all the honor and praise for creating a place to behold such beauty. My eyes saw a lot but my spirit saw much more as I consecrated myself for my journey to the Isle of Patmos.

The Lord used that remarkable isolated island to prepare The Body of CHRIST for the end. Through His humble servant Apostle John, the writings of Revelation were given. There, The Lord revealed what the enemy and the world would do in the last days. Ultimately, it outlines what the Church will go through and the triumphant return of The King.

Women of Valour! Have you read The Book of Revelation? Invest in your spiritual growth and start studying it. Trust me. It's a part of your preparation. To be ready, we must know what GOD knows about the end before the end. BEFORE CNN or Fox News headlines it as breaking news, we need things to be in place. When media starts reporting what GOD already warned about, it'll be too late. Can you imagine the chaos created when billions of people prepare for something all at the same time? Think about supplies. Consider inflation. Remember COVID?

This is the year to manifest end-time preparation!!! Spiritually and Naturally.

Let me share something amazing. December 2023, an intercessor on the Global REVIVALISTS Midnight Prayer line testified she dreamt of a Black Horse. The way she described it, I knew it was the same horse written in Revelation. God was sounding an alarm. He was warning us to engage in URGENT preparation. That unforgettable night, The Holy Spirit, not a news anchor, was giving us The Report of The Lord

I know what the Black Horse means. Do you?

Start studying. Tune Into The Bible. Get Revelation News!

If you're ready, type REVELATION NEWS! or READ ALL ABOUT IT!

"I was in the [a]Spirit [in special communication with the Holy Spirit and empowered to receive and record the revelation from Jesus Christ] on the [b]Lord's Day, and I heard behind me a loud voice like the sound of a trumpet, saying, "Write on a scroll what you see [in this revelation], and send it to the [c]seven churches—to Ephesus and to Smyrna and to Pergamum and to Thyatira and to Sardis and to Philadelphia and to Laodicea"
- **Revelation 1:10-11**

Turkey is a nation I'll never forget. Visiting The Seven Churches in Revelation was a monumental experience for me. Asia Minor came alive as I retraced the footsteps of Apostles John and Paul. I learned so much as I toured with a new believer who Jesus appeared to twice.

Out of The Seven Churches, only Smyrna and Philadelphia were ready for their visitation. The Lord found no fault in them. But the other churches were found wanting and required an overhaul for God's approval. They needed to repent and make corrections.

Although Women of Valour is not a church, we do God's work as one. In 2023, we completed our 7th year in ministry and I can testify God is good and God has blessed. However, I can't take for granted that everything Women of Valour does is fine in His Eyes. I dare not assume that we can go on for another 7 years without making some adjustments. I'm seeking The Lord in an overhaul that will pass His inspection.

During our Women of Valour 2023 Celebration, God revealed some amazing things about our future. Things I have to prepare for personally, corporately, and spiritually. I've decided to see it through the end.

What's The Lord saying to you? Whatever it is make OBEDIENCE a decision. All decisions count. Everyone has a building block for the next one. Ultimately, we'll see the result of our decisions because they always build something.

Apostle Paul, John and others built Churches. What decisions did they make to allow this to happen? We know Paul helped support himself as a tent maker. Sometimes he refused financial help and sometimes he received it to aid his ministry. The lesson here is some decisions change. The YES we gave last year maybe this year's NO.

2024 is The Year of Preparation and Decisions. Seek the Lord in making the right ones.

January

Prophetess Hope McDowell-Gibson

Meet Prophetess Hope McDowell-Gibson

Her Excellency Rev Dr the Honorable Hope McDowell-Gibson, OEA, Th.D, Ph.D.

Prophetess, Revivalist, Senior Pastor, Co-Founder of No Limits Ministries International, Founder & President of HANS TV Network. Dr Hope has purposed to encourage and provide development of creative Leadership to the Body of Christ. Through her Leadership Trainings, Prophetic Mentorship Programs and HANS School Of The Prophets.

Prophetess Hope is a Conference and Motivational Speaker successfully been in the business world for many years and is a seasoned executive coach. She has purposed to train and equip Fivefold Leaders to work in advancing and establishing the Kingdom of God.

Prophetess, is a strong prophetic voice and an End time Prophet, her Ministry is followed by notable signs, wonders and miracles. She is the Author of three books; THE PERSON OF THE HOLY SPIRIT IN YOU, NONE SHALL LACK THEIR MATE and 100% GUARANTEED ANSWERS TO YOUR PRAYERS.

Equipping and Maturing the Saints to Go!

"And He Himself gave some to be apostles, some prophets, some evangelists, and some pastors and teachers, for the equipping of the saints for the work of ministry, for the edifying of the body of Christ, till we all come to the unity of the faith and of the knowledge of the Son of God, to a perfect man, to the measure of the stature of the fullness of Christ."
- Ephesians 4:11-13

This passage clearly describes the functioning of fivefold ministers that were given to the church. (APEST). It is also critical to define the word "equip" as stated in the passage to gain a better understanding of the context of this passage.

The word equip literally means to completely furnish, prepare, make ready and to put into proper condition. In other words, five-fold ministers are called to train and prepare every member of the Body of Christ; to make them effective in what God has called them to do.

Understand, that you cannot be equipped or perfected overnight, the Lord wants to heal you and fill you with His power so that you can do great exploits in advancing and establishing His Kingdom.

It is evident that the church needs a restoration of order and leadership. Sadly, church leaders, who have failed to equip the saints to operate like Christ in character and functionality, will be held accountable on the day of Judgement.

It is crucial and vital for the church to collectively strive to achieve greater accomplishments than Jesus did. The church must collectively perform miraculous signs and wonders, just as Jesus Christ did. This can only be achieved when individuals are equipped to operate in the power of the Holy Spirit, united in carrying out their responsibilities, in the growth of God's kingdom. Utilizing their unique skills and talents, they work together to carry on the mission that Jesus Christ started and even extend it further in terms of impact, and reach.

Notice it is Jesus Christ who gave the apostles, prophets, evangelists, and pastors and teachers to the Body of Christ when He ascended to heaven.

Jesus gave to the church a variety of ministry gifts. In the case of the Fivefold Ministers, they are "Gifts" given to the church. This is so, because the work of the ministry requires these gifts to demonstrate the Power of God. In other words, all believers should grow to become ministers. They must however, all become workers, not spectators! They must become labourers, not viewers!

All believers should be equipped to become Kingdom workers, using the spiritual gifts God has given them. This is in addition to obeying the great commission to all believers to win souls, disciple, baptize and teach them to observe the commands of the Father. (Matthew 28:19-20; Mark 16:15-16).

Yes, we need to be equipped and activated, and THEN sent out to a world in need of what we carry!

Not every believer will serve in the pulpit ministry; some will serve in helps while others in administration.

We see this demonstrated in the early church with the appointment of the seven deacons to support the work of the apostles who were called to teach and train.

Peter made a bold statement saying, "It is not desirable that we should leave the word of God and serve tables. Therefore, brethren, seek out from among you seven men of good reputation, full of the Holy Spirit and wisdom, whom we may appoint over this business; but we will give ourselves continually to prayer and to the ministry of the word" (Acts 6:2-4)

The apostles and the deacons worked together, and the result is seen in Acts 6:7, where it
says, "Then the word of God spread, and the number of the disciples multiplied greatly in Jerusalem, and a great many of the priests were obedient to the faith."

The church today requires all hands on deck. Ministry is not only for the apostles, prophets, evangelists, and pastors and teachers. All believers are ministers. Ministry means service and minister means servant. We need everybody's participation and contribution.

The goal of the five-fold ministers should be to equip believers to do God's work thereby increasing the Kingdom workforce. They are appointed to build up the church and make members functional and effective. Not just well-dressed people who only turn up for Sunday service and then disappear for the remainder of the week only to return for service the following Sunday, but believers who grow in the wisdom and knowledge of the things of the Father, who take their rightful place in the earth as sons of God. These are the same people God depends on to evangelize the world.

Everybody is important and can play a role in the church. Workers are needed in various areas of the church. Are you equipping believers to become Kingdom workers? Are you a Christian worker or spectator? Are you a contributor or only a consumer?

Believers are saved to serve, not saved to be idle in church! They're not saved just to attend church services, go home, and return for another service. God's plan is that every Christian will become a minister, not necessarily become a pastor, or hold an ecclesiastical title.

The scripture reminds us about Jesus "Who gave himself for us, that he might redeem us from all iniquity, and purify unto himself a peculiar people, zealous of good works" (Titus 2:14).

Understand that we are His workmanship, created in Christ Jesus for good works, which God prepared beforehand that we should walk in them.

A Season Refining & Preparation for The Great Harvest!
(Prophecy For 2024)

Last year, September 2023 as I waited on the Lord in preparation for 2024. He spoke in such instructive manner to the Body of Christ saying:

*Many believers will be visited by the Lord in visions & dreams; even loves ones that they are praying for will also be saved through God encounters.

*The Church will be forced to become and operate in the Supernatural.

*There will be pockets of Revival breaking out. (This was shown to me in 2021 before the Asbury Revival in the Universities).

Supernatural Anointing will increase so that many will be laying hands on the sick in the marketplace, the grocery stores and just about everywhere and they will be healed. Keep praying (Acts 10:38) everyday for increased anointing and power.

*There will be major shakings in the Body of Christ, many renown pastors will be asked to step down from office. Some will even die prematurely.

He continued Speaking:

*Prepare the church to reap the "Greatest Harvest "; we have a two-year window.

*Sudden and unexplained death, causing the death toll to rise. Resulting in many being desperate for answers.

*The church will need to seize the moment.

Now the time has come for the Church to rise up. We have been trained for this hour, through mentorship and seminars by anointed ministers. Jesus commissioned the Church to go into the world and preach the gospel; he who is baptized shall be saved.

*It will be a year of judgement in the world.

*There will be immense shaking in the world which will bring judgement on many fronts. This shaking will be a doorway for many to be ushered into the Kingdom of Jesus Christ.

Conversely, there is also a new level of the Glory of God being released during this time.

It's the season of the Greater Glory!

*The shaking will be categorized by double catastrophic events, where different countries will experience similar earthquakes at the same exact time.

The year 24 represents Divine Government and Order, no wonder, you will see the restoration of fivefold ministers where Apostle & Prophets will be setting the church in Divine Alignment & Order.
God always cleanse His House first as explained, the time is come that judgment must begin at the house of God: and if it first begins with us, what then shall the end be of them that obey not the gospel of God? (1 Peter 4:17)

*The shaking will purify the church. As this will remove distractions and thus, brings us to focus by turning our hearts back to Him.

A very chilling and compelling words of the prophet concerning Jesus Christ. He shall sit as a refiner and purifier of silver: and he shall purify the sons of Levi, and purge them as gold and silver, that they may offer unto the Lord an offering in righteousness. (Malachi 3:3)

The heat is on, as there will be a greater level of purging and God will visit the priesthood of the church which is the prayer life of the church. Jesus will sit as a "Refiners Fire" to purge and purify.

As mentioned before, it will be the greatest time to share the gospel of Jesus Christ. Saints, it's not a time to be afraid and hiding in our homes but to be out there witnessing Jesus Christ to the world.

Turn Aside into the Flame

Make A Decision This Year Turn Aside & Focus! There is a requirement for rising up in victory this year. God is saying: "Turn aside into the flame."

Now Moses was pasturing the flock of Jethro his father-in-law, the priest of Midian; and he led the flock to the west side of the wilderness and came to Horeb, the mountain of God. The angel of the LORD appeared to him in a blazing fire from the midst of a bush; and he looked, and behold, the bush was burning with fire, yet the bush was not consumed. So, Moses said, "I must turn aside now and see this marvelous sight, why the bush is not burned up." When the LORD saw that he turned aside to look, God called to him from the midst of the bush, and said, "Moses, Moses!" And he said, "Here I am." Then He said, "Do not come near here; remove your sandals from your feet, for the place on which you are standing is holy ground." (Exodus 3:1-5)

Moses was going about his business, and not only did he sense something, but he also saw something.

He saw a bush that was burning yet not consumed. God has highlighted to me the fact that Moses said, "I must turn aside now and see this marvelous sight." The Scripture then says, "When the Lord saw that he turned aside to look, God called to him from the midst of the bush and said, 'Moses, Moses!"

Imagine, God wanted to speak to Moses. He wanted to anoint Moses. He wanted to commission Moses.

There is commissioning of new mantles that are released but we need to be so sensitive to the Holy Spirit. Notice, that God did not speak to Moses out of the fire until He saw Moses make a "decision" to turn aside towards the bush that was burning.

We are that bush that God wants to burn and consume. The bush represents human frailty, shortcomings, flesh, and weaknesses. God desires to use us, despite our weaknesses, as a conduit for his mighty work. Being consumed, yet not destroyed, speaks to the refining process in which our imperfections and human frailty are set ablaze to reveal the Holy Spirit within us.

There is a sound of revival in the spirit right now!

There is a sound of awakening in the spirit right now!

A cry for the reigniting of fire in the church.
I believe God is looking for those who sense this drawing, who sense this stirring, and who will decide to "turn aside" in this season. What is God doing? He is calling us to turn aside into His flame.
So many believers have become disillusioned, disappointed, and discouraged in this last season.

So many have grown cold and lost hope. Many have even lost vision and become apathetic and complacent. Proverbs 29:18 says, "Where there is no prophetic vision, the people cast off restraint, but blessed is he who keeps the law." Another translation says, "When people do not accept divine guidance, they run wild. But whoever obeys the law is joyful." (NLT)

God is calling us to turn aside from our regular routine. He requires us to move away from our current way of life. He wants us to move our attention away from the difficulties and distractions that have held us back. He is calling us to turn aside into HIS FLAME!

As you begin to turn aside in this season, God is going to set our hearts on fire again. Then, His Glory will be imparted to us when the fire of God is released.

February

Elder Nesa Smith

Meet Elder Nessa Smith

Elder Nesa Smith, a prophetic evangelist, motivational speaker, and author of "The Working Women's Prayer" featured in Lillie Alexander's book, "I Got An Edge," holds various leadership roles. As an ordained Elder and Head Intercessor, she governs alongside the Board of Intercessors at More Than Conquerors Faith Church under Apostle Steve Green's leadership. Additionally, Elder Nesa Smith is a licensed minister, experienced media broadcaster, and co-host of the faith and worship-based program "Reflections of Hope," which aired on WABM television and WAYE radio.

Her impactful journey of ministry spans from the City Hall of Birmingham, AL, to halls of ministry in California, Texas, Ohio, and abroad. With almost three decades of service as a United States government corporate trainer and executive, Elder Smith has received numerous accolades and awards.

Through the inspiration of the Lord Jesus Christ, Elder Smith is the creative force behind the "Rizpah No More Prayer Summit" in Birmingham, AL. This summit uplifts God's people through prayer, agreement, revelation, high praise, and the provision of resources to enhance relationships and prayer life. Elder Smith ministers in the glory and power of God, specializing in empowering individuals to succeed in every aspect of life through God's word, prayer, and communion with Him.

Elder Smith co-hosts the monthly 22-hour call to salvation, "Salvation A Thon," now in its fourth year, with co-host El'Vira Parks and 17 additional team ministers. This initiative, aiming to obey the great commission, leverages social media to reach into every individual's world. Elder Smith also co-hosted "Under an Open Heaven 24 Hours of Prayer Concert," held literally outdoors under an open heaven.

Beyond her public platforms, Elder Smith emphasizes the importance of individual ministry, reaching out to the lost and those in need through hands-on prayers and providing witnessing tools as invitations to Christ. She believes in emulating Christ's love in handling God's precious people, emphasizing that true greatness in the kingdom is found in being a servant.

Residing in Birmingham, Alabama, Elder Nesa Smith is blessed with a beautiful family, including her husband of over 38 years, five children, three daughters-in-loves, and four grandchildren.

The Call to Attention and Honor

In Reverence to the Father, the Lord Jesus Christ, and the Holy Spirit,

I extend my Honor to Apostle Steve Green,

I Honor Dr. Alison Wiley and all Women of Valour.

Some may question the significance of these acknowledgments. It is crucial to establish an order. As the Body of Christ, we must not falter in honoring those who have poured out their efforts, labored, interceded, corrected, provided Kingdom opportunities, and loved us relentlessly. I urge you to allow the Holy Spirit to guide you in acknowledging and honoring those who meet these criteria. In the written word, it may seem like there is movement in various directions, but stay with me. The importance of honor is reciprocal; every seed produces after its own kind. If you only see yourself as the prize, you will only honor yourself. This mirrors the error our adversary made, leading to his expulsion from heaven. I intentionally refrain from uttering his name; too often, he dominates conversations, diverting attention from our Father, Redeemer, Lord, Savior, and the Holy Spirit.

Declare this: I will emphasize the greatness of my Father, Jesus, and the Holy Spirit more than I emphasize my adversary. In Jesus' name.

Beloved of God, Jesus Christ is our ultimate example. He dedicated more time to doing the work than focusing on the enemy. He rebuked the adversary with authority and the Word of God and kept moving in purpose relentlessly.

Truly, our Holy Godhead is too infinite and great to be mentioned alongside a fallen angel whom God will rebuke Himself (Jude 1:9). This brings me to the command I heard in my spirit while contemplating what to write: "Ten Hut!" A militaristic command that brings armed forces to attention. Church of Jesus Christ, Ten Hut, according to Proverbs 4:20 – give attention, be attentive, lean in, and incline your ear to the words of the Lord.

Psalm 1:2-3 states:
"but whose delight is in the law of the LORD, and who meditates on his law day and night. That person is like a tree planted by streams of water, which yields its fruit in season and whose leaf does not wither—whatever they do prospers."

The Word of God is the Source of Intelligence and Hidden Truths:

Consider that denominations in Christianity are liken to branches of service, each with unique functions. The key difference lies in their allegiance – armed forces uphold the constitution of their country, while denominations should be committed to upholding the Constitution of the Word of God. In Christianity, with over 200 denominations nationally and over 45,000 globally, may these fragments unite. Pray for the Body of Jesus Christ to stand as a fortified front, individually and corporately taking their place in God's Commands.

The Word of God is the answer, surpassing man-made wisdom or theology. Again, it holds secrets revealed only to the children of God. A resounding "Ten Hut" echoes in the spirit, calling you to awaken and take your position. You have answered the call and are now pursuing your purpose relentlessly in the will of our Heavenly Father. The training manual (Bible) is open to you, and the Holy Spirit serves as your trainer, revealing things to come (John 16:13).

As we get ready to close…

As we delve into Ezekiel 37, let's recognize that the Word of God is not just wisdom; it is a wellspring of intelligence and concealed truths.

37 The hand of the LORD was upon me, and carried me out in the spirit of the LORD, and set me down in the midst of the valley which was full of bones,
2 And caused me to pass by them round about: and, behold, there were very many in the open valley; and, lo, they were very dry.
3 And he said unto me, Son of man, can these

bones live? And I answered, O Lord GOD, thou knowest.

4 Again he said unto me, Prophesy upon these bones, and say unto them, O ye dry bones, hear the word of the LORD.

5 Thus saith the Lord GOD unto these bones; Behold, I will cause breath to enter into you, and ye shall live:

6 And I will lay sinews upon you, and will bring up flesh upon you, and cover you with skin, and put breath in you, and ye shall live; and ye shall know that I am the LORD.

7 So I prophesied as I was commanded: and as I prophesied, there was a noise, and behold a shaking, and the bones came together, bone to his bone.

8 And when I beheld, lo, the sinews and the flesh came up upon them, and the skin covered them above: but there was no breath in them.

9 Then said he unto me, Prophesy unto the wind, prophesy, son of man, and say to the wind, Thus saith the Lord GOD; Come from the four winds, O breath, and breathe upon these slain, that they may live.

10 So I prophesied as he commanded me, and the breath came into them, and they lived,

and stood up upon their feet, an exceeding great army."

Now, as we close, let us proclaim this prophetic declaration over the churches that open in The Name of Jesus Name:

"I prophesy the Word of the Lord for the Bones of Churches! Oh ye dry lifeless churches live! I prophesy you will not be bitter but saturated with the love of God. I prophesy the Breath of God over every church that opens in the Name of Jesus Christ to receive Euroclydon wind and the breath of God to permeate and resuscitate every member and every church leader. I prophesy to the four winds, O breath, and breathe upon the battered and slain churches that they may live. I Prophesy that you rise in Obedience and Power! I Prophesy an agape love filled church or compassion and anointing. As we prophesied as He commanded, the breath comes into them, and they live and stand up upon their feet and their watch, an exceeding great army."

Take your post, Body of Christ! Honor those who paved the way. Activate the law of reciprocity in honor. In the spirit, hear the resounding "Ten Hut" – attention to what the Spirit is saying.

Pray: Father, I repent for neglecting my post. Ignite in me a desire to honor You in my calling. May I not be self-aware and disobedient. May I glorify You in all I do. Help me, Lord, not to miss You! In Jesus' name. Amen.

In today's self-centric society, I prophesy that the Church is on a forceful advance. We are going nowhere as long as Jesus tarries!

As it is in Heaven so Shall it be here on earth in Jesus Name!

Compassion A Conduit of Movement

Contemplating crucial decisions and the importance of readiness, my thoughts turn towards the elements in Christ that sparked miracles, signs, wonders, provisions, refreshing's, healings, defying human reasoning, and even raising the dead. I've compiled relevant scripture references, and I encourage you to delve into them. Within these verses lies a common element essential for operating in the realms where Jesus himself operated. Let's explore the Word together and observe the transformative impact when compassion is in action. Before delving into the verses, let's establish a biblical understanding of compassion.

In Hebrew, "Rakhum" is the term for compassionate, literally translating to "womb." While we often associate the womb with the female anatomy for nurturing and conceiving babies, biblically, compassion extends beyond this physical aspect—it is a profound empathy for something with a heartbeat.

According to the dictionary, compassion is defined as the emotional response that arises when confronted with another's suffering, motivating one to alleviate that suffering. Remarkably, this description aligns with our Compassionate Saviour, who, in His earthly form, entered the world through the womb of a woman, countering the effects of fallen humanity.

Let's dive into the scriptures together, as they speak to various aspects of this profound concept.

Matthew 14:14-21 Matthew 14:14-21 King James Version

14 And Jesus went forth, and saw a great multitude, and was moved with compassion toward them, and he healed their sick.
15 And when it was evening, his disciples came to him, saying, This is a desert place, and the time is now past; send the multitude away, that they may go into the villages, and buy themselves victuals.
16 But Jesus said unto them, They need not depart; give ye them to eat.

17 And they say unto him, We have here but five loaves, and two fishes.
18 He said, Bring them hither to me.
19 And he commanded the multitude to sit down on the grass, and took the five loaves, and the two fishes, and looking up to heaven, he blessed, and brake, and gave the loaves to his disciples, and the disciples to the multitude.
20 And they did all eat, and were filled: and they took up of the fragments that remained twelve baskets full.
21 And they that had eaten were about five thousand men, beside women and children.

Matthew 15:32-38 Matthew 15:32-38
King James Version

32 Then Jesus called his disciples unto him, and said, I have compassion on the multitude, because they continue with me now three days, and have nothing to eat: and I will not send them away fasting, lest they faint in the way.
33 And his disciples say unto him, Whence should we have so much bread in the wilderness, as to fill so great a multitude?

34 And Jesus saith unto them, How many loaves have ye? And they said, Seven, and a few little fishes.
35 And he commanded the multitude to sit down on the ground.
36 And he took the seven loaves and the fishes, and gave thanks, and brake them, and gave to his disciples, and the disciples to the multitude.
37 And they did all eat, and were filled: and they took up of the broken meat that was left seven baskets full.
38 And they that did eat were four thousand men, beside women and children.

Matthew 20:29-34 Matthew 20:29-34 King James Version

29 And as they departed from Jericho, a great multitude followed him.
30 And, behold, two blind men sitting by the way side, when they heard that Jesus passed by, cried out, saying, Have mercy on us, O Lord, thou son of David.
31 And the multitude rebuked them, because they should hold their peace: but they cried

the more, saying, Have mercy on us, O Lord, thou son of David.

32 And Jesus stood still, and called them, and said, What will ye that I shall do unto you?

33 They say unto him, Lord, that our eyes may be opened.

34 So Jesus had compassion on them, and touched their eyes: and immediately their eyes received sight, and they followed him.

Mark 1:40-41 Mark 1:40-41
King James Version

40 And there came a leper to him, beseeching him, and kneeling down to him, and saying unto him, If thou wilt, thou canst make me clean.

41 And Jesus, moved with compassion, put forth his hand, and touched him, and saith unto him, I will; be thou clean.

Luke 7:11-13 11 And it came to pass the day after, that he went into a city called Nain; and many of his disciples went with him, and much people.

12 Now when he came nigh to the gate of the city, behold, there was a dead man carried out, the only son of his mother, and she was a widow: and much people of the city was with her.

13 And when the Lord saw her, he had compassion on her, and said unto her, Weep not.

14 And he came and touched the bier: and they that bare him stood still. And he said, Young man, I say unto thee, Arise.

15 And he that was dead sat up, and began to speak. And he delivered him to his mother.

16 And there came a fear on all: and they glorified God, saying, That a great prophet is risen up among us; and, That God hath visited his people.

Mark 6:34
King James Version

34 And Jesus, when he came out, saw much people, and was moved with compassion toward them, because they were as sheep not having a shepherd: and he began to teach them many things.

As we immerse ourselves in the scriptures, a clear pattern emerges – when our Savior was stirred with compassion, miracles unfolded.

The crucial query arises: How can the collective body of believers tap into these realms of miraculous occurrences? It appears that compassion is not merely an option but a fundamental necessity for the Body of Christ. Could it be that the absence of compassion is a missing component in our faith?

The Word emphasizes that the synergy of reading God's Word and being moved with compassion results in tangible manifestations. For the body to authentically reflect Christ, compassion must be embraced as a non-negotiable. Without this vital element, our actions may fall short of the transformative movements demonstrated by Christ during His earthly ministry.

A yearning for compassion becomes imperative, a desire to witness God's people saved, delivered, healed, and even raised from the dead, regardless of popularity. True compassion, when aligned with the Spirit of the living God, becomes a catalyst for provision, a conduit for healings, a force that transcends human logic, and a guiding light for those who are lost. Compassion resurrected and continues to raise the dead.

Even the most eloquent speaker, the influential politician, or the aesthetically pleasing individual, without compassion, remains devoid of true power. Oratory skills without compassion are mere intellectual exercises, political influence lacks substance, and physical beauty without compassion lacks genuine impact.

In this pivotal moment, God is issuing a call to the Body of Christ—an invitation to wield true power. This power manifests when we, as individuals and as a collective, are genuinely moved with COMPASSION.

I want to leave you with this one scripture. Please read it out loud if Possible.

Lamentations 3:22
King James Version

22 It is of the LORD's mercies that we are not consumed, because his compassions fail not.

We have everlasting compassions from the Father that will never fail or give out.

Prayer: Baptize your body again in your ways of compassion. May we be moved with it so that your Spirit will move miraculously.
Finally, this is a heart positioning. Allow Holy Spirit to extricate and heal anything that will hinder compassion.

As it is in Heaven so shall it be on earth!
Lord, Let YOUR Kingdom Come to Us.

Cut Throat!

In the pursuit of divine guidance, a message resonates with the Spirit—a phrase: "cut throat," linked to gluttony. This echoes Proverbs 23, urging us to pay attention when dining with rulers and cautioning those given to appetite to put a knife to their throat. It's clear that God is not advocating self-harm but emphasizing the gravity of uncontrolled appetites, potentially leading to destructive outcomes.

Reflecting on an open vision years ago, I vividly recall witnessing the spirit of gluttony. In this vision, it resembled the green hue of the Mucinex emoji, for a lack of better words, a snot representative, with boils, incessantly consuming without cessation. It prompted the realization that demonic influences subtly infiltrate our media, presenting evil in grotesque forms directly in our face. These visuals, once internalized and or downloaded, can be used to disturb and distress believers and their children. By affecting their dreams with nightmares, increasing fear, and bombarding their minds.

Returning to the theme of appetite, I recognize the significance of that vision in curbing overeating. It served as a revelation, shedding light on the adversary's tactics. The correlation with the first sin involving food and disobedience in Genesis 3:6 is evident.

Eve's misinterpretation and misrepresentation of God's command led Adam to commit High Treason, of which Adam gave away the earth. Please don't miss the fact that the power of agreement was evident even in the garden. Resulting in the separation between humanity and God—a veil. The question arises: Could our fork and spoon symbolize a barrier between us and God? Disobeying the promptings of the Holy Spirit might indeed be yielding to the enemy's voice. Again, this is not a small thing. This principle extends beyond food, influencing every facet of our lives.

The Genesis narrative highlights the impact of what Eve saw—lies from the adversary, evident in the adversary's advertisement, making the forbidden fruit more enticing.

This parallels the constant bombardment of appealing images in our daily lives. Guarding our eyes and ears, the gateways to our souls, is emphasized to thwart the enemy's tactics.

Living a fasted life brings our flesh under subjection to the Holy Ghost, sensitizing us to the Spirit, resetting our bodies, and breaking yokes. It empowers us against the "this kind spirits," as referenced by Jesus in Mark 9, which fasting and prayer alone can combat.

May we align ourselves with God's will, prospering and being in health as our souls prosper (3 John 2).

Pray with us: Father in Jesus Name we come in repentance for not following divine guidance in our eating habits and all areas of life. We renounce any demonic download we ignorantly allowed. Anoint us afresh, cleanse us, and cover us with the Blood of Jesus. May we yield to the Holy Spirit. In Jesus Name, Thank You!

Note: A sidebar mentions a blog, "The Spiritual Warfare Blog," offering detailed insights into topics like the demonic origins of Pokémon.

As it is in Heaven, so let it be here on earth. Lord Jesus, Thy Kingdom come.

March

Dr. Althea Winifred

Meet Dr. Althea Winifred

Dr. Althea Winifred is not just a woman on the move; she is a Woman of God. She is an Evangelist, Prophetess, and Teacher of the God's word. She is also a writer, author, and businesswoman.

Bermudian born and did her primary schooling at Francis Patton and attended Prospect Secondary School for Girls for a few months. She left
Bermuda with her parents and did her high school in Ottawa, Canada, and all college or university degrees and achievements in United States of America.

Her Education:
Dr. Althea has a bachelor's degree in business administration with emphasis in Management. She has a master's in religious education. She has an earned Doctorate Degree in Philosophy of Theology and has an Honorary Doctorate degree in Theology. She is a Preparation Coach, and an author of over 21 plus books, devotionals, articles.

She is also Colonial Chaplain in 2014, and in 2016 became a Regional Vice Chancellor, and in 2018, she was appointed as a Professor for CICA- International University and Seminary. She will be awarded a Certification as a Christian Counsellor with emphasis in Mental Health and hopes to start her own Counselling Clinic. In 2024, She was asked to be a writer for Women of Valour Month Calendar for the Month of March

Her Ministry & Mandate:
An inspirational and motivational speaker known nationally and internationally, she is Founder and Director of Ministries of Substance established by God in 1996. In July 1996 she was birth W.O.R.K. (Women of Royalty for the Kingdom) is her Women's Ministry. Dr. Althea's mandate is to make ready and prepare a people unto the Lord and help women to be **P.E.A.R.Ls** (Prepared, Progressive, Encouraged, Equipped, Effective, Authentic, Resilient, and Loyal) and being like our God in pouring out Love no ma]er what life put before us.

In 2006 she started Daughters of Substance. In addition, in 2014, Dr. Althea started Substance International Institute Faith School, name changed in 2018 to Substance Institute offering quality and affordable online classes to students who want to achieve a Biblical Education for God's assignment.

In December 2023 – The vision for the Prophetic Fire Prayer Movement was birth and was launch in January 2024 in McDonough, Georgia. She is the host of "Confirming The Word" program being launch different social media platforms.

Her Slogan:
Her slogan since 1996 is "Living by Faith and not by Facts yet stating my Facts and waiting in Faith!" She is known as a Woman of Substance with integrity and has proven FIA (Faith In Action because her Faith Is Active). Dr. Althea firmly believes in the Father, Son and Holy Spirit and stands on the Word of the Lord; knowing, that God is God whether the answer is Yes, No or Wait.

Her Favorite Scripture:
Her favorite scripture is Ezekiel 12:28 ~ "Therefore say unto them, thus saith the Lord God; there shall none of my words be prolonged (postponed) anymore, but the word which I have spoken shall be done, saith the Lord God".

She knows that people come into our lives for a reason, a season, or a lifetime. She has only one opportunity to impact them for an eternity.

She has a heart after, and for God, wanting all to be saved and none to perish. She knows all relationships are worth saving, but not all relationships want to be saved!

Her Family:
She is the Mum to two children, and Grand Mum to two grandchildren.

"The Foundation of Preparation"
Topic: Preparing Your Heart

Scripture: Proverbs 16:1

"The preparations of the heart in man, and the answer of the tongue, is from the Lord."

Words of Encouragement:
Dear Woman of Valour, as we embark on this journey through the year of preparation and decision, let us begin with the most crucial step: preparing our hearts. In the hustle and bustle of life's demands, the quiet preparation of our hearts often takes a back seat. Yet, it's in the stillness, in the quiet moments of surrender, where true preparation begins. The wisdom of Proverbs reminds us that our plans, words, and decisions find their best foundation when they are aligned with the heart God has prepared.

Preparing your heart is an act of faith, a declaration that you trust in God's plan for your life more than your own. It's a daily commitment to listen before speaking, to seek before deciding, and to trust before acting. This preparation doesn't mean you'll always know the way forward. Rather, it means you'll be aligned to the One who does.

Imagine your heart as fertile ground. Just as a gardener prepares the soil before planting, so must we prepare our hearts for what God intends to sow within them. This involves uprooting the weeds of doubt, fear, and pride, and cultivating the soil with prayer, Scripture, and obedience. As you do this, you'll find your decisions rooted not in the fleeting whims of the world but in the eternal wisdom of God.

As women of valour, we are called to be both warriors and nurturers, fighting the good fight of faith while tenderly caring for the hearts God has entrusted to us, starting with our own. Let this year be marked by a heart fully prepared for whatever God has in store, knowing that a heart aligned with His is the most powerful tool in making decisions that honor Him.

Prayer:
Heavenly Father, we come before You, seeking to prepare our hearts as fertile ground for Your Word and will. Guide us in this season of preparation and decision-making, that we may seek You above all.

Help us to cultivate hearts that are ready to receive Your direction and strong enough to follow it, even when the path is unclear. In Jesus' name, Amen.

"Decisive Faith"
Topic: *Walking by Faith, Not by Sight*

Scripture: 2 Corinthians 5:7

"For we walk by faith, not by sight:"

Words of Encouragement:

In a world that prizes certainty and visibility, walking by faith presents a divine paradox. To walk by faith, not by sight, is to move forward based on confidence in what we cannot see, rather than what we can. This year, as we focus on preparation and decision, let's embrace the challenge of walking by faith.

Walking by faith means making decisions that might not make sense to others or even to ourselves at times. It's choosing to trust in God's promises, even when the evidence suggests otherwise. It's stepping out of the boat, like Peter, keeping our eyes fixed on Jesus, and believing He will hold us up.

But how do we cultivate this decisive faith? It begins in the secret place, in the deep, quiet moments spent in God's presence.
 It's nurtured by immersing ourselves in Scripture, where we're reminded of God's faithfulness to those who dared to believe Him at His word. It's strengthened in community, where we can encourage one another to take steps of faith.

As women of valour, we are no strangers to the call to be courageous. Yet, true courage is not the absence of fear; it's the decision to move forward in faith despite the fear. This year let's make decisions not based on what we can see with our physical eyes but on what we know to be true in the spiritual realm. Let's prepare our hearts to responsive to the gentle leading of the Holy Spirit, trusting that what He guides us to do, He will also provide for.

Remember, the most significant moments in Scripture came when ordinary people made the decision to trust God's word over their understanding. As you face decisions this year, big and small, may you do so with a faith that is bold, decisive, and rooted in the eternal truth of God's word.

Prayer:
Lord, grant us the courage to walk by faith and not by sight. In this year of preparation and decision, help us to trust in Your unseen hand guiding us, Your voice leading us, and Your promises sustaining us. May our decisions reflect our trust in You, and may our lives be a testament to the power of faith in action. Amen.

"Courageous Decisions"
Topic: Embracing Courageous Choices

Scripture: Joshua 1:9

"Have not I commanded thee? Be strong and of a good courage; be not afraid, neither be thou dismayed: for the Lord thy God is with thee whithersoever thou goest."

Words of Encouragement:
The path of preparation and decision is often lined with moments that require courage beyond our natural ability. Joshua 1:9 isn't just a comforting reassurance; it's a divine command to be strong and courageous. This command comes with the promise that we are not alone; God is with us wherever we go.

Making courageous decisions means stepping beyond the boundaries of our comfort zones, facing the unknown with faith instead of fear. It involves making choices that align with God's will, even when they go against the grain of societal expectations or personal convenience.

Courageous decisions often require us to stand alone, to speak out when it's easier to remain silent, and to act when inaction would be the safer choice.

As women of valour, we draw our courage not from our own strength but from the Lord, who promises to be with us. This year let's lean into that promise. Let's make decisions that may seem daunting but are rooted in the conviction that God's way is the best way. Whether it's a change in career, a move to a new city, standing up for what's right, or simply choosing to trust God in the face of uncertainty, let's do so with the courage that comes from knowing He is with us.

Let's also remember that our courageous decisions can inspire others to step out in faith. As we lead by example, let our lives be a testament to the power of living courageously for Christ.

Prayer:

Lord, infuse us with Your strength and courage as we face decisions that require us to trust You deeply. Remind us that we do not walk this path alone but with You by our side. Help us to make choices that reflect Your bravery, love, and truth, and may our lives inspire others to live courageously. In Jesus' name, Amen.

April

Evangelist

Wilma Walker

Meet Evangelist Wilma Walker

Evangelist Wilma Walker Lives in Washington County Texas, part of Brenham Texas, she's married to Rev. Richard Walker. They both serve as associate Ministers of the Gospel of New Beginnings Missionary Baptist Church under the Leadership of Pastor Artis Edwards Sr, in the City of Brenham Texas.

Evangelist Wilma answered her call to preach the Gospel in 2002, and preached her first message in August of 200 where she received her License to preach under the Leadership of Pastor James Mable Sr. of the Missionary Camp Baptist Church in Navasota Texas. In the Month of December 2019, she received her ordination license as an Evangelist and became a Five Fold Ministry leader as an Evangelist. She also serves as leader of the intercessor team and teacher of Sunday School and Bible study. Evangelist Walker also serves as assistant program coordinator on the board of Living for Christ Ministries.

Evangelist Walker is the proud mother of one biological son ,(Jacquay) and one precious granddaughter (Jaliyah Michelle) She also shares her love with five daughters and four sons embracing them as her own.

Evangelist is an Anointed Woman of God , and has a Love and compassion for preaching and teaching the word of God to equip and encourage others. Evangelist Walker believes in the Supernatural Power of God, her favorite scripture is Romans 8:28, And we know all things work together for good to them that love God, to them who are the call according to His purpose.

God Can Handle It

Can you imagine waking up making preparations for the day? As you look into the mirror, you see troubles of life staring at you. Your job, your children, your spouse, life issues surrounding you,

Well let me tell you being a Christian doesn't exempt you from trouble according to (John 16:33) Jesus warned us of great difficulty in this life and in this world. He reminds us that we will have trouble,, but he says take heart! I have already overcome the world,,

The Apostle Paul also reminds us not to be anxious about anything but in every situation by prayer and petition with thanksgiving, present our request to God and 1 Peter 5:7 says cast all your cares on him!!

Give it to God. Remember God can Handle it!!

So take a deep breath and start brushing your teeth. Then start saying out loud, Thank you Lord I know you can handle it. Believe you have what you say as it says in Mark 11:23 and experience the Peace of God

We praise God who cause his power to work in us. In the way he is able to do much more than we, could even think about, We want everyone to know how Great is our God!!

Yes!!! He can Handle it!!

Battered and Bruised to Be Bold

"For many if not most of us, it takes a crisis before we really believe. It takes the loss of a job, a problem with a marriage, a difficulty with a child, a debilitating illness or injury or a dependence upon some form of addiction to turn us around and cause us to change. It is when we come to that place where we cannot pull it off, we cannot seem to cope or we cannot make victory happen, then we truly reflect and respond to his call. It is we are overwhelmed by events of the day, when our sins far exceed our blessings, when life has beaten us down, drawn us out, emptied us of what we think we are and convinced us of our worthlessness that we come to know Jesus."
-Psalms 65:2-4

When life has battered us bruised us, beaten us up and broken us, that is when we finally find that we can be bold in His power.

When we are at the end of our rope and all we have left is Jesus, that is when we find Him.

When we have run out of options and we have nothing of ourselves left to give up, we find our Savior. When Jesus comes he lifts us up. We finally begin to trust him when we have nothing else. The burdens of the past become stepping stones for building a future. We are exhausted and fall upon our face to praise Him , because he is all we have and we finally realize he's all we need and that He is enough.

God is a present, watching and waiting for us to finally give up and call upon Him, Remember he is there when we need Him, we can depend totally upon Him.

Preparation Time

Preparation means a readiness to proceed . It means a foundation has been set to build upon. How ready are you to receive what you have been asking God for? Have you made the necessary preparations? Is your heart right towards your enemies? Is your heart right towards God ?

One of the ways we prepare as believers is we must put on the whole armor of God and then after that pray and watch. Some have suited up but stopped looking. They may have watched but stopped praying. All of these are necessary to be prepared for what's coming to us in battle or blessings.

Ephesians 6:13-18

13. Therefore take up the whole armor of God, that you may be able to withstand in the evil day and having done all to stand 14. Stand therefore having girded your waist with truth , having put on the breastplate of righteousness, 15. Having shod your feet the preparation of the gospel of peace ,16. Above all taking the shield of faith which you will be able to quench all the fiery darts of the wicked one 17. And take the helmet of salvation, the sword of the spirit which is the word of God ; 18. Praying always with all prayer and supplication for all saints.

When you prepare in the manner required, you can be steadfast and unmovable to abound in the work of God. Sometimes our decisions don't prove our readiness. Our decisions may prove we failed to pray or failed to gird up in truth. We may have failed to put on the righteousness of God which causes us to choose sin. This leaves our chest and backs uncovered which exposes us and opens us up for attacks.

Joshua 24:15

(15) And if it seems evil to you to serve the Lord, choose for yourselves this day whom you will serve, whether the gods which your fathers served that were on the other side of the River, or the gods the Amorites, in whose land you will dwell, But as for me and my House we will serve the Lord.

When you have prepared you have laid the foundation, every decision stands before you. You will be able to stand on the truth of righteousness , firmly set your salvation which is Jesus Christ , sowing the Gospel everywhere your feet tread , remembering that if his peace is not in it, you're not around peace.

Covered with faith and armed with the word of God, every decision is no longer a point of anxiety or fear, but it is an opportunity for God's handiwork and Glory to be revealed through you .

Are you prepared for the blessings? Are you prepared for his return ? What decisions are preparing you for your purpose on earth??

May

Michelle Smith

Meet Michelle Smith

Michelle P. Smith is a native New Orleanian who currently resides In Houston, Texas. She is a wife and mother and is honored to serve in ministry at the Windsor Village Church Family.

She is a dance minister who expresses the Word of God through movement and also ministers the Word of God when invited as a speaker.

She leads an intercessory prayer group, Called to the Closet, through which she offers mentorship and coaching in the area of prayer and hosts prayer gatherings. Through Michelle P. Smith Ministries, she hosts annual gatherings for visionaries where they are inspired, ignited, equipped and activated in the work of the Lord.

Michelle P. Smith has hosted Vision board gatherings and workshops over the course of the last decade, helping attendees to express and accomplish their God-given vision.

Professionally, she is the Owner and Hair Stylist at International Coiffure Salon. She has been a licensed hairstylist for 18 years helping her clients to have stylish, healthy hair.

She is honored to express the love of God through serving His people.

Jesus laments for... Jerusalem

"O Jerusalem, Jerusalem, the one who kills the prophets and stones those who are sent to her! How often I wanted to gather your children together, as a hen gathers her chicks under her wings, but you were not willing! See! Your house is left to you desolate; for I say to you, you shall see Me no more till you say, 'Blessed is He who comes in the name of the Lord!"
- Matthew 27:37-39

Jesus cries out on behalf of Jerusalem because He knows the trouble that they will see soon. Even though He desires for them to see mercy, He knows that there is a way that they must go in order to see the prophecies fulfilled. He also cries out for the hearts of the people in the city. They have grown cold and insensitive to the voice of God, as He has spoken through His prophets. They are not willing to hear the ones who are sent to warn of the things to come.

Let us #CryOut for... Our Cities, States and

Nations

We must cry out in prayer for the peoples' ears and eyes to be open to what God is saying in this hour. The remnant must gather and "Cry aloud, spare not, lift up thy voice like a trumpet, and shew my people their transgression, and the house of Jacob their sins." (Isaiah 58:1). It is not a time for silence or quiet contemplation. It is time to lift up our voices and weep between the porch and the altar (Joel 2:17) praying that those who have ears to hear and eyes to see will be attentive to the season that we are in. And that we will indeed see the salvation of the Lord.

Jesus laments from… the cross

Matthew 27:45-46

From the sixth hour until the ninth hour darkness came over all the land. About the ninth hour Jesus cried out in a loud voice, "Eli, Eli, lema sabachthani?" which means, "My God, My God, why have You forsaken Me?"

Jesus Cries out to His Father from a place of deep despair and agony. Jesus had never known a time of separation from God. But in that moment, as He took on the sins of the world, He felt forsaken and abandoned by Father God. So many emotions probably flooded Jesus in that moment-worry, anxiety, fear, sadness, grief. The list could go on and on because it is the list of how we feel when we are separated from God, our Father.

Let us #CryOut from… the cross that we must bear

When we have experienced times of deep sadness and grief, there may be the tendency to either suppress what we are feeling or completely ignore it. But as we look at our perfect example, Jesus, He acknowledged the pain and even hopelessness that He was experiencing in the moment. We cannot deny that in this human experience we will go through some challenging times, however, as we have seen, when we cry out, God hears and answers.

Let Us #CryOut

Cry Out for Redemption

"I will go before you and will level the mountains (to make the crooked places straight); I will break in pieces the doors of bronze and cut asunder the bars of iron."
- Isaiah 45: 2 AMPC

In Psalm 26, David is crying out to Adonai for redemption of his reputation. He is one who walks in integrity before the Lord. He declares his innocence symbolically by washing his hands and coming to the altar (Psalm 26:6). David is giving God his resume of righteousness. He has walked faithfully in the truth of the Lord (Psalm 26:3). He does not sit with deceitful men or hypocrites (Psalm 26:4). Instead, he is found in the habitation of the house of the Lord (Psalm 26:8).

David requests of Adonai…

#<u>Vindicate</u> me

To vindicate means to free from allegation or

blame and to protect from attack or encroachment. David looked to God for protection from any allegation his enemies could hurl at him. He understood the importance of an excellent character and good reputation. He also knew that when the attacks and allegations would come that His Sovereign Lord would be the one to defend him and set the record straight. David did not have to plead his own case. As he cries out to God he will be cleared of blame and guilt.

Psalm 26:1 (AMP)

Vindicate me, O Lord, for I have walked in my integrity; I have [relied on and] trusted [confidently] in the Lord without wavering and I shall not slip.

#Examine me

The Lord examines David's heart as though He was examining gold. He looked for impurities that would give the enemies legal grounds to attack David's character. God inspected his heart closely to test the condition and status of David's inner man.

David is found as a man after God's own heart.

Psalm 26:2 (KJV)

Examine me, O LORD, and prove me; try my reins and my heart.

#Test me

Not only does David submit to the examination of the Lord, but he also submits to the testing. Testing here implies that the Lord is proving that David is a person of integrity and that David is worthy of carrying out what God has designed. Only God knows the true intentions of the heart and only He can test the heart in a way that will reveal true motives.

Psalm 26:2

Put me on trial, LORD, and cross-examine me. Test my motives and my heart.

#**Redeem** me

The Lord is the One who redeems. David is keenly aware of his need for redemption, and he knows that he cannot do it for himself. In His grace and mercy, He redeems us and restores us to our rightful place in Him and we are established as victorious over our enemies.

Psalm 26:11

But as for me, I shall walk in my integrity; Redeem me and be merciful and gracious to me.

As we submit to the examination and the testing of the Lord, He will redeem us and we will see vindication from those who come against us. Let us Cry Out!!!

Hallelujah!

Cry Out for Rescue

Adonai does not delay, when it comes to rescuing His loved ones! He sends His help quickly to those who cry out to Him. Psalm 70 is a reminder that God will rescue you. He will free you from the imminent danger presented by your enemies. Those who seek to destroy your reputation and sully your name will be disgraced. The trap that they have set for you they, themselves, will fall into. They will reap the harvest of the seeds of confusion that they have sown. And you will declare, "God is Great and Glorious!"

#Seek God and be Glad; Take **#Joy** in the Lord; God is your **#help** and **#Rescue**

Seek the Lord with all diligence. Strive after Him that He may be found. Even in the presence of your pursuer, God will make you glad because you know Him as the One who rescues. Fear cannot catch you, nor can it overtake you because you are moving with God. His gladness in you makes your feet swift and your steps sure. Your enemies are confused by the gladness and joy that you have as they try to destroy you. As you seek the Lord, He will be your strength and your peace, even in the presence of those who make rude comments about you and mock you. The joy of the Lord will, indeed, be your strength. Do not relinquish the peace that God has given you. In the face of those who seek your life, God will be your ever-present help and He will rescue you.

Psalm 70:4-5
May all those who seek You [as life's first priority] rejoice and be glad in You;
May those who love Your salvation say continually, "Let God be magnified!"
But I am afflicted and needy; Come quickly to me, O God! You are my help and my rescuer; O Lord, do not delay.

Hallelujah!!!

June

Lady Tammy Stewart

Meet Lady Tammy Stewart

Tammy Stewart, affectionately known as Lady T in her ministry, serves with compassion as a midwife in coaching and mentoring women to discover their Divine purpose.

Tammy earned her Bachelor's degree in Psychology from Houston Baptist University and is currently completing her Master's in Counseling.

As the leading lady of Greater Emmanuel Family Worship Center, Tammy has faithfully served alongside her husband, Bishop Titus Stewart, for nearly 25 years.

Gifted in the creative arts, Tammy writes plays, poems, worship songs, and productions. She is also the founder of Motivated to Motivate, LLC, a Certified Life Coach, Co-founder of TB Stewart Ministries, Owner of O'Rose Boutique, and an author.

Passionate about inspiring and speaking life on both religious and corporate platforms, Tammy ministers with a blend of spiritual and practical strategies that break strongholds and empower individuals to walk in their God-given authority, leading to Kingdom expansion.

Tammy enjoys traveling, spending time with her family, fostering individual growth, working out, and living and abundant life. She is the proud mother of Trenton (married to Yasmine) and BiBi to her granddaughter, Trinity, and soon-to-be grandson.

Decision Making

Have you ever made decisions that you've later regretted? Perhaps at the time, you didn't have the wisdom or tools needed to make sound choices. Here's another question: Have those decisions cost you in ways that still affect you today? I know I've been there.

The truth is, making decisions is one of the most challenging tasks for many people. However, the Creator designed our brains to navigate this process. The prefrontal cortex, a crucial part of the brain, oversees judgment, decision making, problem solving, emotional control, and memory. Remember, God designed our brains with purpose and intentionality.

Proverbs 3:5-6:
"Trust in the Lord with all your b heart and lean not on your own understanding; in all your ways submit to him, and he will make your paths straight."

This passage encourages us to rely on God's

wisdom and guidance rather than our own understanding, reminding us to seek His direction in every decision we make.

As I carry out my earthly Kingdom assignment, I've realized that one of the ways God uses me is to bring clarity to others. Over the next three days, I'll provide tips, grounded in biblical principles, on what to consider before making decisions. Today, we lay the foundation, and tomorrow, we'll dive deeper.

PRAYER:
Heavenly Father, we come before You with humble hearts, seeking Your guidance and wisdom for the next three days. As we explore the principles of decision making, let Your Word illuminate our minds and guide our steps. Grant us clarity, understanding, and the discernment to align our choices with Your will. May Your Spirit lead us, and may our decisions bring glory to Your name. In Jesus' name, we pray. Amen.

"The prudent see danger and take refuge, but the simple keep going and pay the penalty."
- Proverbs 27:12 (NIV)

Preparation is a necessary part of living wisely. Proverbs 27:12, contrasting the responses of the prudent and the simple to danger that was forthcoming. The prudent (sensible) person, recognizing potential risks, takes refuge. However, the simple person continues on their path, that causes them to face the consequences of the danger that was seen.

This verse teaches us that wisdom involves foresight and action. It's not enough to merely see danger; we must take steps to protect ourselves and those we love.

We prepare spiritually. In our spiritual lives, preparation means staying steadfast in prayer and reading the Word of God, equipping ourselves to face trials and temptations. Jesus often withdrew to pray, preparing His spirit for the challenges ahead. Similarly, we must nurture our relationship with God daily, finding refuge in His presence.

In addition, practical preparation is a necessity as well. In our daily lives, this wisdom might manifest in financial planning, career development, or health maintenance. Are we saving for the future, acquiring new skills, or maintaining a healthy lifestyle? The prudent person foresees potential hardships and prepares accordingly, ensuring stability and resilience.

Remember, preparation is an act of wisdom, and it is often the difference between thriving and merely surviving.

PRAYER:
Lord, grant us the wisdom to see the dangers ahead and the courage to take refuge in You. Help us to prepare in all areas of our lives, trusting that as we take prudent steps, You are our ultimate refuge and strength. In Jesus' name, we pray. Amen

"Put your outdoor work in order and get your fields ready; after that, build your house."
- Proverbs 24:27 (NIV)

A couple of years ago, I decided to get fit "again." Filled with enthusiasm, I set out to do a HIIT run—a high-intensity interval training exercise involving alternating sprints and jogs. On that fateful day, I neglected the essential step of stretching and warming up my muscles. As I took off sprinting, an intense pain hit my leg, sending me crashing to the ground. I had fractured my ACL and couldn't train for 8 weeks. Why? Because I refused to prepare before taking off.

This experience taught me a profound lesson about the necessity of preparation. Just as physical exercise demands warming up and conditioning, our spiritual lives require careful preparation to avoid setbacks and ensure success. The Bible stresses the importance of preparation, reminding us that it is a key element in fulfilling our God-given purpose.

Proverbs 24:27 advises us to put our outdoor work in order before building our house. This wisdom translates to our spiritual journey as well. Before we can build a strong spiritual foundation, we must prepare our hearts and minds. This preparation involves regular prayer, diligent study of God's Word, and seeking His guidance in all we do.

The injury of my ACL was a direct result of skipping preparation. Ignoring our spiritual preparation can lead to spiritual injuries such as burnout, yielding to fleshly desires, or a weakened faith. Just as my body needed stretching to endure the HIIT run, our spirits need conditioning to withstand the challenges and temptations of life.

Preparation allows us to face challenges without falling apart, to get up quickly from setbacks, and to stay focused on our goals.

PRAYER:
Father, we thank You for the wisdom of preparation. Help us to understand the importance of preparing our hearts and minds for the journey of faith. Give us the discipline

to invest time in prayer, study, and seeking Your guidance. Protect us from the pitfalls of rushing ahead without proper preparation. In Jesus' name. Amen

PROPHETIC WORD:

I have you in preparation mode. What may feel to you as oversight by men is Me developing you before sending you. Yes, your work will be great, but you cannot be successful if you're unprepared. Don't be weary in preparation, I will soon release you before great men. You will sit before kings, you will stand on great(er) platforms. Don't be weary. Am I not God?

July

Sharonda Thomas

Meet Sharonda Thomas

Sharonda Thomas's life is rooted in faith and family. She and her husband, Gerald, have shared a loving marriage and partnership for 20 years. Together they are raising three amazing boys. She has also been blessed to be a part of raising her two bonus sons and now gets the chance to bask in the joy of loving their five.

Sharonda has an Associate of Arts and Business degree and is currently pursuing her bachelor's degree in accounting. She is also certified in religious education and counseling.

From leading songs in the church choir at the age of four to delivering her first sermon at sixteen, Sharonda's spiritual journey has shaped her into a leader in her community. She is trained in prophetic worship and loves to lead people into God's presence.

She serves as the pastor and co-founder of Kairos Harvest Ministry HUB in Richmond, TX, where she leads alongside Gerald. Together, they lead weekly Bible studies and fourth Sunday "Acts House" worship services, helping equip believers for the end times.

Beyond her ministry, Sharonda is a passionate entrepreneur. She runs a bookkeeping service and loves to create creative projects through her company, Creative Space and Grace. She is gifted in events and designs and uses that gift to help people from all walks of life create memorable events with Opulence Events & Designs. Sharonda is passionate about God, her family, community service, and entrepreneurship. She believes in empowering others and building strong, healthy relationships.

Be Prepared for The Shift

"Daniel answered and said: "Blessed be the name of God forever and ever, to whom belong wisdom and might. He changes times and seasons; he removes kings and sets up kings; he gives wisdom to the wise and knowledge to those who have understanding; he reveals deep and hidden things; he knows what is in the darkness, and the light dwells with him."
- Daniel 2:20-22 ESV

In my quiet time and preparation for this month, I heard the Lord say #ShiftChange! He's shifting people, places, and things in and out of our lives. He is shifting closed doors to open doors. He is shifting the old and the new.

In a #shiftchange, the old gives way to the new. The exhausted worker who has worked 8-12 hours moves out of the way and turns the load over to the more energized and refreshed worker. Vital intel about what has happened on the current shift is given to the one taking over the new shift. The new worker may come in with new methods and strategies, but nothing can be implemented without intel given by the current worker.

#CatchThis: The passing and receiving of intelligence #OpenDoors for the new and fresh!

Here's the point: As things change in our world and kings are removed and kings are being set up, do not shift your focus from the basics—go back to your first love! Remain in HIM! Grieve what was and move on quickly!

- Prepare for extreme obedience!

- Decide now that you will not be shaken!

- Prepare to remain steadfast!

- Be prepared to be completely authentic with Father.

- Be prepared spiritually and naturally!

- Prepare now not to rely on your own strength but the strength of our strong tower!

Welcome to the **#ShiftChange**! Blessed be the name of the Lord forever and ever!

Be Prepared for Sevenfold Repayment! #ShiftChange

There may have been times when you did not pray as intentionally as you should have. There may have been moments when you did not proactively utilize the weapons that God gave you to defeat the enemy. There may have been moments where you did not fully operate in your gift and placed it on the shelf for later. There's no judgment! Only warning: the enemy is viscous and jealous of who you are and what the Lord has given you, that he can never have. Be aware, he may have snuck into your house and stolen what belongs to you.

"The thief comes only to steal and kill and destroy. I came that they may have life and have it abundantly." John 10:10 ESV

Do not worry or fret! The Lord is shifting the abundance into your hands. Father says I hear your cry! I hear you saying, "There's there is not enough to make ends meet and prepare!" Do not be afraid, what Father calls us to, He pays for!

"But when he (the thief) is found(caught), he must repay seven times [what he stole]; He must give all the property of his house [if necessary to meet his fine]." Proverbs 6:31 AMP

Some versions of Proverbs 6:31 say, "If," but I like this version, which translates to, "When he is found." The good news is that he has been found, and repayment is yours. He must repay you what he stole seven times plus give you whatever he has in his house!!

- Are your affairs in order?

- Where will you keep the repayment?

- Do you have room for overflow?

- Have you prepared for abundance?

Amos 9:13MSG *"It will happen so fast our heads will swim"*

We are in the seventh month, and he is completing and perfecting some things concerning us! Prepare for the abundance and the overflow! When Father repays us sevenfold, it will be completion! There is no space for waste! We must know what we are to do and how we are to move for the Kingdom. Know this: As an Ambassador of Heaven, this abundance and overflow is not only for you to live your best life, but it is for the Glory of God and for the Kingdom of God!

This repayment is for something greater than us! We must ask God for the <u>#Strategy</u> of Joseph, the <u>#Courage</u> of David, and the <u>#Wisdom</u> of Solomon to carry out the assignment. When the Lord trusts you, extreme obedience is necessary!

Prepare! Prepare! Prepare!

Shift In Perspective

Elisha replied to her, "How can I help you? Tell me, what do you have in your house?"

"Your servant has nothing there at all," she said, "except a small jar of olive oil."
- 2 Kings 4:2

In times of famine, stress from what we perceive as a lack in all areas can cause panic and anger! In the climate that we are now living in, we see the results of it everywhere: in our physical and mental health, in our finances, in our jobs, and even when we drive on the roads. It's evident that our world is changing. America is changing.

Do not be alarmed by what you see but be encouraged by what you do not see! What we see is temporary and can change in an instant, but what we do not see is eternal and everlasting.

2 Kings 4 tells the story of the widow woman and her two sons. Although she needed to

borrow vessels to hold the oil, the miracle she needed was already in her house. She only needed a place to pour the excess oil. The prophet Elijah shifted her perspective to see that she had more than enough in the Lord's hands!

If you are looking for a miracle, don't stop looking! I would encourage you to shift your perspective! Your miracle is in your house! YOU are the miracle in your house! You are the vessel that will house the oil that will flow until God is done! The gifts and talents Father has invested in you will carry you through any and every famine!

Check for excess (excess is your "except for a small jar of olive oil.") Ask yourself, "What has God poured into me?" and "What do I already have in my house?"

Spiritually: Check for unused gifts and talents. Check for dormant dreams. Check for unwritten visions. Check for confession of lack. Check the heart for wrong motives.

Naturally: Check your bank accounts for

excess spending, your pantry for excess staples, and your closet for excess clothing.

Checking for excess shifts our perspectives from lack to more than enough. We will find that God has caused the oil to continue to flow!!

August

Jennifer Lewin

Meet Jennifer Lewin

Jennifer Lewin is an acclaimed gospel artist known for her soul-stirring vocals and heartfelt lyrics. She is a passionate worshipper who has been in music ministry from the tender age of 6.

Born and raised in Canada, She began her journey in a children's choir and has served in ministry since then. She is a GMA Canada Nominated and Award winning independent artist.

Her Debut Album hit #1 on the iTunes Charts within 24 hours of its release and was nominated for a Juno Award in the category of Contemporary Christian Gospel album of the year.

Jennifer's original music and heart for worship has garnered national and international attention over the past couple years, she has been invited to minister all across Canada and several nations in Africa; Ghana, Nigeria, Kenya, South Africa. She has also travelled to the islands of the Caribbean as well as a the USA.

Jennifer is a mentor and founder of "Nay- O - Me" Networks, a mentorship program for young women in ministry and is also the founder of Worship Without Walls, a weekly street ministry worship experience in Toronto.

Jennifer is an entrepreneur and ordained minister

but above all of that; she is a servant who is working very hard to get the messages of love and restoration out to as many as possible.

Scripture: Ephesians 3:20

20 Now to him who is able to do immeasurably more than all we ask or imagine, according to his power that is at work within us. 21 to him be glory in the church and in Christ Jesus throughout all generations, for ever and ever! Amen.

Devotion:

Even the most powerful of machines need to at some point get connected to a power source. There is a power working on the inside of you and it's crucial for you to stay connected to your Source. He's more than able but it is according to the power that is working within us... The power to believe, the power to pray, the power to wait, the power to trust completely in His plan. Really connect with Him today.

Declaration:

Father, in Jesus Name, I confess that you are not just my saviour but You are my Source. I can't do anything without You. You are where all of my help comes from. Let my mind stay connected, let my will be connected, let my body be connected to You, stir up the power within me.

Song Selection: "He's Able" By: Detrick Haddon

Scripture: Daniel 2:20-23

20 Daniel answered and said:
"Blessed be the name of God forever and ever, For wisdom and might are His.
21 And He changes the times and the seasons; He removes kings and raises up kings; He gives wisdom to the wise And knowledge to those who have understanding. 22 He reveals deep and secret things; He knows what is in the darkness, And light dwells with Him.
23 "I thank You and praise You,
O God of my fathers; You have given me wisdom and might, And have now made known to me what we asked of You, For You have made known to us the king's demand."

Devotion:
God is above the natural time and speed of man. There is nothing that you are waiting on that is outside of His reach. He has times and seasons in His hands, He is not governed by time. In this season may The Lord grant you even more access into greater revelation about gracefully waiting and the

understanding of times and seasons.

Declaration:
OH, God, You are Alpha and Omega. You are the beginning and the ending. You hold time and seasons in your Capable Hands. I declare today, I not only trust You, I trust Your timing.

Song Selection: "Be Still and Know" By: Travis Greene

Scripture: Psalms 108:1-5

*1. My heart, O God, is steadfast;
I will sing and make music with all my
soul. 2 Awake, harp and lyre!
I will awaken the dawn. 3 I will praise you,
Lord, among the nations; I will sing of you
among the peoples. 4 For great is your
love, higher than the heavens; your
faithfulness reaches to the skies.
5 Be exalted, O God, above the heavens; let
your glory be over all the earth.*

Devotion:
There is nothing and no one that can be compared to the glory of God. Everything about Him is high above us. Meditate on His love and
faithfulness today.

Declaration:
My Lord and My God, I declare that your love is at work in my life. I see how you are making difficult things easy, how you soften the hearts of people. May I walk in your

love today, let someone see your love at work in me today.

Song Suggestion: "Be Lifted" MOG

September

Prophetess Tashana Pearson

Meet Prophetess Tashana Pearson

Prophetess Tashana Pearson Prophetess Tashana Pearson is a dedicated servant of God with a powerful testimony of redemption and faith.

Her journey with the Lord began at the age of eleven, following a profound encounter that set the course for her life. Though she faced periods of struggle, including a period of homelessness, God's grace continually drew her back to His house and His presence.

Throughout her life, Prophetess Tashana has maintained an intimate relationship with the Father, walking and talking with Him as if He were always in her midst. Despite numerous challenges and opposition, her unwavering desire has always been to witness and participate in greater works of God. Called to this pivotal moment in history,

Prophetess Tashana is committed to rooting out, pulling down, and declaring the Word of God. Her ministry is characterized by prophetic insight, deliverance, and, most notably, a profound gift of intercessory prayer. Through her fervent prayers, many lives have been healed and transformed, fulfilling God's purposes on Earth. Prophetess

Tashana is blessed to be married to Elmore Pearson, her steadfast partner and support, and is the proud mother of two sons, Rahiem and Elmore, and the grandmother of 5. All are the joy of her life.

She has spearheaded numerous 12–24-hour prayer watches that have resulted in significant spiritual breakthroughs and global impacts. In addition to her prophetic and intercessory ministry, she holds a Bachelor of Science in Health Information Management and Health Technology and has served as a marketplace prophet, offering counsel to CEOs and entrepreneurs. Prophetess Tashana also owns Tashana Closet Boutique, Leg-A-See Healing Balm and Candles, and has authored a prayer manual. She travels across the nation, preaching and teaching the Gospel, guiding others to discover and walk in their God-given destiny. Her ultimate mission is to reveal the transformative power of a relationship with the Father to the world.

Ordained as a Prophetess by Bishop and Apostle Cannon at the Cathedral of the Holy Spirit at Living Word Christian Center in Augusta and affirmed by Bishop William and Naomi Martin at City of David Christian Center her leaders.

Spiritual Forensic

In the mentorship class with Apostle Lisa James, "spiritual forensics" was discussed, emphasizing the importance of changing one's mindset to overcome obstacles. This concept parallels military training, where soldiers push their limits to build resilience.

Joshua 7:6-9 serves as a foundation for this approach. After the defeat at Ai, Joshua and the elders of Israel sought God's understanding and guidance about what had gone wrong. This reflects the practice of reflecting on setbacks to gain insight and improve future outcomes.

Spiritual forensics involves celebrating victories and examining what was lost or learned from failures. Proverbs 15:22 highlights the value of seeking counsel: "Without counsel, plans fail, but with many advisers, they succeed." By reflecting on past experiences and understanding mistakes, you can better prepare for new challenges and move forward more effectively.

Prayer:

Heavenly Father,

I come before You, acknowledging the good times and the battles I have faced. I realize there have been moments when I missed Your guidance or failed to recognize pitfalls. I ask for Your help to reveal any errors in my life so I can prepare for the next season You have planned for me.

Please guide me in understanding both my successes and my mistakes so I can walk uprightly before You. I seek Your wisdom and counsel in all my plans and directions for life. As Proverbs 15:22 says, "Without counsel, plans fail, but with many advisers they succeed."

Help me to reflect on and learn from my experiences. As Proverbs 24:6 reminds us, "For by wise guidance you can wage your war, and in an abundance of counselors there is victory."

Thank You for this new season. I am committed to preparing myself and emerging stronger and better through Your guidance.

In Jesus' name!

Year 5785

As we transition into the year 5785, we move into a new phase of grace and favor. This year symbolizes the completion of past efforts and fulfillment (7) while also ushering in new beginnings and opportunities (enhanced by God's grace (5).

In preparing for this new season, recognize that while it brings blessings and fresh starts, there will still be challenges. Drawing on your reflections from past experiences, be ready to navigate potential pitfalls with the wisdom gained from previous spiritual forensics (no more repeating cycles because we have self-awareness). Embrace the grace and favor of this new year while staying mindful of the lessons learned to ensure a successful and transformative journey.

Heavenly Father,

Thank You for guiding us into the new year of Rosh Hashanah and the season of 5785, marked by new beginnings and Your grace. I ask that you cover me and everyone who reads this passage. Protect us from falling into the pitfalls of our past and help us embrace this new season with confidence.

As challenges and distractions arise, keep us focused on You. Let us recognize and receive the blessings You have prepared for us. We come against any spirit of self-sabotage that might hinder our progress. Surround us with Your protection and prepare our hearts and minds to fully embrace the abundance You offer, blessings without sorrow. Thank you, Lord, for pushing back the gates of hell that cannot prevail against us... THIS IS OUR WINNING SEASON. In Jesus' name, Amen.

Prophetic Instructions: Today, in your devotion time, write out your desires and give them to God.

Fully Baked

I want to honor, everyone that reads this and every leader that has imparted in me over the years. The Lord is Kind. Thank you to the photographer, Malachi Easley, Dr. Allison Wiley, Bishop William and Naomi Martin, my husband, my children, and grands and most of all God for being my Father.

I have been seeking the Lord for understanding about the state of the church and why we aren't seeing the miracles and possessing the promises as we should. The answer is quite simple. Many of us struggle to trust God fully, so we attempt to make things happen on our own, missing the essence of childlike faith He calls us to embody. Jesus said in Matthew 18:3, "Truly I tell you, unless you turn and become like children, you will never enter the kingdom of heaven." This childlike faith means depending on God just as a child depends on their parent for care and provision.

Because we often fail to trust Him and rely on the Holy Spirit within us, we resemble

Ephraim, described as "a cake not turned" in Hosea 7:8. Just as a half-baked cake is incomplete and flawed, so too are we when we don't fully embrace the process of transformation God intends for us. Imagine being that cake, pleading, "Lord, the oven is too hot; take me out!" Yet, the heat of the oven is crucial for transformation, changing ingredients from their raw state into a finished product.

In the same way, if we allow the Father to fully process and transform us, though the journey may be challenging, the result will be worthwhile. We will not be a half-baked offering but a product of endurance and divine craftsmanship, capable of nourishing others. As Philippians 1:6 assures us, "He who began a good work in you will carry it on to completion until the day of Christ Jesus."

Prayer:

Father, I thank You for Your love and discipline as You refine and process me. I desire to be whole, complete, and lacking nothing. I cry out for Your mercy, asking You not to let me remain half-baked like Ephraim. Your Word promises that You who began a good work in me are faithful to complete it. Finish what You have started in us. We give You permission to mold and transform us so that we may be effective change agents for Your kingdom. We praise Your holy name for the newness You are bringing into our lives in this season. Let Your will be done, not ours. Amen.

October

Reverend Sharnelle Jones

Meet Reverend Sharnelle Jones

Reverend Sharnelle is an energetic personality, passionate preacher, prayer warrior and educator.

She is the Founder of "Prayer, Ministry, ACTION! Pray it Out!" of Houston, Texas, sharing powerful prayer strategies and exegetical Biblical teachings for persons with careers and dual callings in ministry. Prayer, Ministry, ACTION! Schedules Silent Prayer Retreats, workshops using the Spiritual Disciplines that help believers to pull back the layers of pain, stagnation that can weigh believers down and drag them underneath what God has in store for their lives.

"Prayer, Ministry, ACTION", through the guidance and direction of the Holy Spirit, holds uplifting prayer gatherings including Praying on Monday Nights, Pray it Out, Rest and Fire, My House Shall Be Called a House of Prayer, Women Who Slay and most recently, B.R.A.I.D.S (Being Ready and Innovative for Daily Success!) - a prayer strategy group for 11-12 year-old girls.

"Prayer requires honesty - whether you are thrilled or depressed, pray it all out to the Lord! Jesus is advocating this help for you! Lay what is heavy in your heart and mind before the throne of God. The heaviness says, 'You're too weighed down to pray; just get on with your day.' Tell God what the heaviness said. YOU belong to God!"

A native of Beaumont, Texas, with Louisiana roots and a large family, Sharnelle received her Bachelor of Sociology and Music from Texas Southern University. She graduated from Houston Graduate School of Theology with a Masters in Divinity (Cum Lade) and was awarded the St. Nicholas Foundation for Excellence in Ethics Award. Sharnelle by occupation is a Head Choir Director and Award-Winning Educator in the Pasadena Independent School District (Texas) for over 20 years.

Sharnelle was a contributing devotional writer for "Overflow Magazine", Women of

Valor 2019 Inspirational Calendar Leader and preaches at conferences as the Lord leads. An associate clergy at The Luke Church under the Pastoral Leadership of Dr. Timothy Sloan in Humble, Texas, Sharnelle was one of two women making history at The Luke Church in 2017 as one of the first women ordained in the ministry of the church's one hundred seventeen year history!

Sharnelle is the blessed and thankful wife to Marcus Jones of 31 years, the super proud, loving Mother to Hannah and Joshua, and "G-Mommy" to Willow. I love being with and around my #Jones4! The Lord grace gifted us with amazing children who love the Lord.

"So Moses returned to the Lord and said, 'Oh, what a terrible sin these people have committed. They have made gods of gold for themselves. But now, if you will only forgive their sin—but if not, erase my name from the record you have written!"
- Exodus 32:31-32

BUT GOD, WAIT!

Our Great God, today we come before you with reverence for You and You only. We need Your Glory. We stand today solemnly asking your forgiveness and pleading for another chance over a people and a nation and a church that could no longer wait for Your servant and thus made their own idols, fashioned their own gods and said, "Now these are the reasons for our great success."

MOSES. Intercession in its Biblical form is actually quite dangerous. Intercession in its organic form can mean a loss of life for the one interceding. God says, "My fierce anger will blaze against them" and tells Moses to leave so that God can destroy them but the

Intercessor stays anyway and says, "But God, wait…" That is dangerous! Moses, instead of charging out of the way, remains between the God in fierce, blazing anger and the people below who are dropping it like it's hot! Moses, starts pleading and actually pacifying God with questions and reminders. After Moses's position and plea God changes God's mind! My Lord!

Then Moses climbs the mountain a second time just to pray for forgiveness for Aaron and the people and even puts his life on the line: Yahweh, if you won't forgive them then erase my name from the record! If God would have destroyed the nation, to live the remaining days of his life with the memory of only their sin and their destruction would be too much to bear! What would have happened to the nation of Israel if Moses would have jumped out of the way? What would have been the legacy of God to Egypt if God would have destroyed His own freed people? (Moses asked God this question). Intercession involves questions (tough ones), considerations, and remaining in the danger zone until God says, "I've changed my mind."

BUT GOD, WAIT! Oh dear, intercessors! Today as you are led to pray and cover this nation, your nation, may you carry within you the compassion of Christ to pray, seek God's mercy and plead for another chance! Send up "reminders!" Point to Christ and His ultimate atonement! I know that like the people at the bottom of the mountain, many are rambunctious, fleshly, idol worshippers, turned away from God, say they are followers but are bowing to other gods, but climb your prayer mountain one more time! Be reminded that Jesus died on another "hill" once and for all! Point your prayers to the fulfillment of Christ!! This next destruction of the Lord is too much to carry! May the Lord have mercy! Have mercy, Lord! Have mercy, Lord!

Arise! Shine! The Lord Shall Get This Done!"

A Mighty fortress is our God! Glory to God today!! The hands the Lord gave you are the hands that will be lifted up before the LORD! The mouth that God gave you is the mouth that will bless the Lord, tell of the Lord's Goodness, spread and share the Good News and sing the new song of the Lord!! Hallelujah!

"Arise, shine; For your light has come!

And the glory of the Lord is risen upon you." Isaiah 60:1 (NKJV)

"Don't you know?" the angel asked. "No, my lord," I replied. Then he said to me, "This is what the Lord says to Zerubbabel: It is not by force nor by strength, but by my Spirit, says the Lord of Heaven's Armies. Nothing, not even a mighty mountain, will stand in Zerubbabel's way;" Zechariah 4:6-7 [A] (NLT)

ARISE! The Lord is already risen within you!

The NASB says "dawned upon you." Risen in this Hebraic context means the glory is abiding in you, applied to your life; calling your life, carrying you. In the Assyrian/Arabic it means "returned to you."

My God! Women of Valor, get up! No matter the test, the glory of the Lord is not impacted, reduced or clearance racked based upon your current state - it's based upon God and Who God is!! If you've been beaten down by tests and storms and temptations, the glory is being returned to you! God has the plan for your life and it shall be established - not by your might, nor by your power (nor your connections or experienced rejections) but by the Spirit of God shall it happen! The terms "risen" and "dawn" mean apparent, blazing, guiding the way! If you want to see the sun you aim in that direction! If you want sunshine you simply go outdoors or open the windows! There is no doubt of the power of God upon you, the wisdom, knowledge, choices, planning, outcomes, move, counsel, glow and action coming out of your life!!

The Glory of the Lord is RISEN WITHIN -

no need to seek outward for this! Lord, how shall I get this done? Don't you know? SHINE!! Amen!!!

Fixed Hour Prayer

Thanks be unto You, God, for You giveth us the victory through Christ Jesus! We bless you this Monday! We enter into this day with thankfulness unto Your Name, for You are a Good God!!! My God…

This is the day to cover your family before the Lord! Before Jesus chose the twelve disciples, Jesus prayed all night long. "All night long" is a 12-hour shift. The Late Reinhard Bonke says, "Twelve hours…that's one hour for every disciple." Cover your family in the Word of God and pray them out before the throne of God! Fixed Hour Prayer is prayers lifted up before God at specific times, developing the ability to hear a word from God in the midst of daily activities, and places you "in the wheel in the middle of the wheel," in the pulse of the Holy Spirit of God! Set a timer to sound at the top of every hour and stop for one to fifteen minutes to pray specifically for your family.

HOUR ONE: "But as for me and my family,

we will serve the Lord." Joshua 24:15 Pray that each member of your family will serve the Lord! Hallelujah! Pray for the salvation today and future salvation of your family. Pray that the love of God with the whole heart will be the lives for your children, marriage or if you are single. Call out the names of each family member. Anchor them in prayer. They will not serve or worship the gods/thoughts of this culture (popularity, mediocrity, minimalist, average, etc.) but they will CHOOSE, in every year of their lives, to serve the Lord! Regardless of age, they shall be saved! (*Note: please do not avoid this. Do not say, "Well, they're grown; they do what they want to do." This sounds like tiredness from wrestling with your children. Keep in mind that your prayers are going to the Ever-present God! I have witnessed in my own life children who went left, but the fervent prayers of parents kept them from untimely deaths, accidents and trauma. Prayers can go where conversations cannot!)

HOUR TWO: "For the Lord is good; his mercy is everlasting; and his truth endureth to all generations." Psalm 100:5 (KJV)

At the top of the second hour, pray the Goodness of the Lord over your family. If you are single, stand in your prayer ground, anoint yourself with oil and declare this verse over your life! If you are married, pray for the Everlasting, mercy of the Lord and His Forever enduring TRUTH over your children, grandchildren, and great-great-great-great grandchildren! For the Goodness of the Lord over _____ _____ ___. God's truth endures over _____, _____! For every generation that is to come may the Goodness of the Lord endure over my family and the truth of Lord ENDURE, ENDURE, ENDURE over them! Name the decades: ____, ____, ____, ____, ____, ____! Lord, your Goodness and truth will never run out from my family, in the powerful Name of Jesus! Repeat this prayer all throughout the hour.

HOUR THREE: "A final word: Be strong in the Lord and in his mighty power." Ephesians 6:10. Loosey-goosey faith is not going to cut it in this hour! Pray for the Lord to hold your family. No paralyzing fear in your family! Pray that your family will stand strong against the wiles of the devil! Pray that your family will know the truth about the Lord Jesus and receive the wisdom, direction and knowledge of the truth of God at all times! Pray for strength at all times, at all levels, for all choices and all knowledge at all times! Pray that when storms come their way that their faith will not waiver. Pray over friendships, unspoken hurt, their confidence to lead, resistance in their lives that attempt to shut down their prayer times. Pray against false doctrines and false gospels that will lead them blindly into a ditch! Pray for your family to resist grudges and walk speedily in forgiveness so that God can use them! Call out each name and pray as the Holy Spirit leads you!

Repeat these prayers at the top of the hour. Listen to what the Lord is telling you about each family member and the generations to come. Cover also your housekeepers and lawn servicer, anyone who comes regularly to your home, add them to these prayers. This is your new reality of God's presence in all times in all things! Amen!

November

Dr. Allison Wiley

Christians Are Called To Lead Nations To Christ

In their lifetime, Elijah and Elisha were known as The Chariots of Israel because they steered Israel back to GOD. These holy men were needed as ungodly rulers were misleading God's people into idolatry.

"How long will you be of two opinions?" said Elijah. How long will you choose both sides? You must choose today who you'll stand with. Either the gods of Ahab and Jezebel or the GOD of Elijah.

Women of Valour! How long will Christians go to church BUT not stand with it on election day? How long will Christians play both sides?

Tomorrow we'll know where America is in its greatest decision. Tomorrow we'll see which god our nation has chosen.

Prays UP !! for a righteous win.

"So the king gave the command, and they brought Daniel and cast him into the den of lions. But the king spoke, saying to Daniel, "Your God, whom you serve continually, He will deliver you."
- Daniel 6:16

I'm seeing BIG promotions occurring in spaces of opposition. Literally...I'm seeing Godly recognition under fierce accusations.

My GOD! Those who are making righteous decisions are being prepared, promoted, enlarged, and positioned in highly visible places to share The Good News of The Kingdom.

It feels like the era of Daniel. A man who prayed even though he was ordered not to.

Faced with death, Daniel chose God's righteous commands above man's unrighteous laws. What did God do? HE showed up with signs and wonders, shut the mouths of the lions, saved Daniel, and prospered him in the reign of two Kings.

There are dens of devouring lions roaring against our Christian values, but as we serve GOD, HE WILL DELIVER US FROM THEM ALL

Be proud to be a Christian Women of Valour. Decide to stand and take ground. GOD will rescue you.

JESUS CHRIST LIVES FOREVER

"He heals the brokenhearted And binds up their wounds."
- Psalm 147:3

Today I'm praying for you. From a place within you that may be hidden. So many are making decisions from a wounded place. You know God's Word but you choose erroneously because you're hurting.

There's an old saying "Hurt people hurt other others" Sadly, this is true. Many negative cycles can be traced to someone who hurt us.

Know this! Being controlled by your emotions rather than The Holy Spirit can lead to disobedience. Disobedience leads to compromise. Compromise leads to unrighteous living. Unrighteous living hinders the full power of The Holy Spirit in your life. When you're bleeding or broken, the focus becomes you rather than The Lord's need for you to forgive and surrender.

Get healed. Be set free. God loves you and wants to restore you. Prepare for an emotional breakthrough!

My prayers are with you.

December

Elder Patricia Wright

Meet Elder Patricia Wright

The life of Elder Patricia R. Wright began in Kansas City, Kansas. At the young age of 16, she was saved and trusted her life to the Lord. Being part of a local church, she served in many capacities and ministries including Sunday School teacher, YPWW president, secretary, and an usher board and choir member to name a few.

After moving to Texas in 1982, she was involved with several ministries but was ordained as an Elder in July 2012 under the leadership of her current Pastors, Apostle Dr. Albert & Prophetess Marcelia Anderson of Breath of Life International Ministries.

The ministry that she stewards, Rosebud Ministries, was birthed in August 2012 after a dream regarding the book of Acts chapter 6. With the encouragement of her Pastors, the following December 2013, Rosebud Ministries held its first meeting. Rosebud continues to serve widows and other women who have experienced loss both locally and throughout the United States. With a growing

Facebook and YouTube audience, she continues to spread the message of hope, empowerment, and restoration by hosting community outreach events.

Elder Wright has served on other prayer platforms as well as Women of Valour since 2019. She is also a business owner, a certified Christian counselor, a Chaplain, and a Texas Notary. Her three adult children and four grandchildren bring her much joy as she surrounds herself with a vast collection of plants and lots of music!

> "Strength and dignity are her clothing, and she laughs at the days to come."
> - Proverbs 31:25

As we enter the second week of December, let's take a moment to pause and share a laugh. Entrusting our lives, along with all our dreams and aspirations to Yahweh is the safest choice we can make. As we transition from this year to the next, we acknowledge that uncertainty lies ahead.

The past year, 2024, serves as a reminder that we are not in control; Yahweh is. No one could have predicted the events and outcomes of this year, and we can't foresee what the future holds either. However, we can embrace the new year without fear if we believe in our Father.

A woman of noble character knows her source of strength each day. She balances truth and grace through her relationship with Yeshua and wraps herself in Yahweh's goodness. Her strong relationship with her Creator empowers her to laugh at the days ahead.

Let go of the need to control life; instead, embrace the life that Yahweh has given you. This time of year is perfect for reflecting on what you want to carry into the new year and what you desire to leave behind. If you have an issue that is causing division in your relationship with Yahweh, it's time to let it go.

Focus on developing a new mindset that will bring you joy. You can choose joy; and lead with laughter in the coming year because you chose the Master. Instead of focusing on your fears and apprehensions, clothe yourself in the sovereignty of Yahweh and laugh out loud.

"So we built the wall, and the entire wall was joined together up to half of it, for the people had a heart to work."

- Nehemiah 4:6

What I love about today's scripture is its emphasis on the collective effort. As we approach the end of 2024, let's ask the Father to instill in us a heart to work. We have projects that need to be initiated and completed for the advancement of the Kingdom.

As WOV, let's remain open and attentive as the Holy Spirit guides us into new projects for the upcoming year. There is so much Kingdom work to be done—new territories to explore, greater horizons to witness, and more souls to be saved. While building projects and expansions require physical effort, Nehemiah reminds us that the people had a heart to work. Ultimately, the true work begins in our hearts.

Philippians 2:13 tells us, "For it is Elohim who is working in you, both to desire and to work for His good pleasure." The Father is at work within us, empowering us to carry out His work.

Father, let the work begin in our hearts and then extend to our hands and feet.

"And I shall give you the keys of the reign of the heavens, and whatever you bind on earth shall be having been bound in the heavens, and whatever you loosen on earth shall be having been loosened in the heavens."
- Mat 16:19

Recently, our congregation has been exploring the subject of the Kingdom in depth. While there is much to discuss, I would like to pose a question to WOV and others: How can we use the keys to the Kingdom that Yahweh has given us more effectively?

The verse mentioned refers to the keys of the Kingdom that we possess. We have the ability to open what is necessary and to lock up what needs to be restricted here on earth, knowing that it will also be bound or loosed in heaven. When Yeshua entrusted us with these keys, He also granted us the authority to use them wisely—to secure what is important and to unchain what is meant to be open and free.

This means we hold the key to permanently lock away any past pain, disappointment, lies, or betrayal that has troubled many of us for so long. Similarly, we can use these keys to unlock and release joy, strength, vision, and other blessings from the heavenly realm. So, grab the keys and exercise your Kingdom right! #keystothekingdom